MINNES

WILDLIFE

impressions

Farcountry
PRESS

Photography and text by **Dominique Braud**

ABOVE: The early light of an April morning catches a male sharp-tailed grouse in full courtship display on his traditional dancing ground, known as a lek.

RIGHT: Cougar sightings are extremely rare in Minnesota but have increased in recent years. It is not known if Minnesota has a resident population or if the individuals sighted are wanderers from western states or escaped pets.

FRONT COVER: A cow moose feeds on lily pads in the Boundary Waters Canoe Area Wilderness. Moose have no fear of reaching underwater to find aquatic vegetation growing at the bottom of lakes and ponds.

BACK COVER: A fly impudently sits on a female loon's head while she incubates her eggs. Minnesota, with its many lakes, is host to more common loons than any other state except Alaska.

TITLE PAGE: Trumpeter swans squabble on the Mississippi River on a bitterly cold winter morning, surrounded by unconcerned Canada geese. Trumpeter swans are the largest waterfowl in Minnesota.

ISBN 10: 1-56037-482-9
ISBN 13: 978-1-56037-482-4

© 2008 by Farcountry Press
Photography © 2008 by Dominique Braud

For more information about our books, write Farcountry Press, P.O. Box 5630, Helena, MT 59604; call (800) 821-3874; or visit www.farcountrypress.com.

Created, produced, and designed in the United States.
Printed in China.

Feigning injury, a killdeer does a "broken wing" act to lure a predator away from its nest.

INTRODUCTION

by Dominique Braud

My childhood was shared between the high desert plateaus of North Africa—where my dad, a career officer, was fighting a futile war in Algeria—and the peaceful, sparsely populated Limousin region of south-central France. Both instilled in me a deeply rooted love for wild, wide-open spaces, and the greatest disdain for tame, fenced-in landscapes.

Fortunately for me, I found some of the wildest places on earth when I moved to Minnesota almost thirty years ago. I felt instantly at home here. Sure, the linguistic familiarity I had with the many French names of rivers, lakes, counties, parks, and cities that pepper the state map may have had something to do with that. Left behind by intrepid explorers and voyageurs who mapped the region and harvested its bounty of beaver pelts, these names are reminders of a time when France's far-reaching influence on the globe extended to Minnesota before it was sold to the United States as part of the Louisiana Purchase in 1803.

Certainly some of its original habitats have been plowed under, drained, or logged, but the love that Minnesotans have for their natural environment is palpable, along with the commitment to preserve it in parks, refuges, and preserves. The state is endowed with one national park (Voyageurs), two national monuments (Pipestone and Grand Portage), two national forests (Chippewa and Superior), thirteen national wildlife refuges, fifty-eight state forests, seventy-two state parks, and the crown jewel, the incomparable 1.3 million-acre Boundary Waters Canoe Area Wilderness that encompasses and protects more than 1,000 lakes.

Approximately 8,000 square miles of the state's 87,000 square miles are covered by water. Water reigns supreme here; boating, canoeing, and fishing are a way of life. Even the name and nickname of the state underline the supremacy of water: "Minnesota" is derived from a Lakota word meaning "sky-tinted water." To be sure, there is plenty of sky to be reflected in the "Land of 10,000 Lakes" (although there are actually about 12,000 lakes of ten acres or more), most of the lakebeds gouged out eons ago by gigantic glaciers that gripped the entire Upper Midwest.

Mightiest of all is Lake Superior ("Gitchi-Gumi" or "Great Water" for the Ojibwe), which borders Minnesota from Duluth to the Canadian border. It is so deep and large—2,900 cubic miles—that it could accommodate all the other Great Lakes, with room for three more the size of Lake Erie. Two major rivers, the scenic St. Croix and the Minnesota, empty into the legendary Mississippi,

Two young white-tailed bucks lock antlers in a pre-rut contest. Whitetails are one of Minnesotans' favorite big-game animals and are found in every county in the state. Their numbers exceed one million.

whose headwaters can be found at Lake Itasca, in Clearwater County.

This abundant water is a magnet for wildlife. Minnesota's numerous lakes, streams, and rivers teem with 158 species of fish that provide world-class sport fishing for bass, northern pike, walleye, and muskellunge. Recreational fishing generates $1.58 billion in revenues for the state annually.

Ten million acres of wetlands (the most found in the United States after Alaska) provide feeding and nesting grounds for countless waterfowl, shorebirds, songbirds, and raptors. Trumpeter swans, Canada geese, ducks, cranes, herons, pelicans, and eagles use the Mississippi Flyway during their fall and spring migrations.

And what about the land? Minnesota's three major biomes support eighty species of mammals, twenty-one species of amphibians, and twenty-nine species of reptiles; 226 species of birds nest here. Occupying much of the northeastern tier of the

state, including the watery maze of the Boundary Waters Canoe Area, extensive coniferous forests mix with birch and aspen to form the northern boreal forest, home to the elusive lynx, as well as bald eagles, moose, beavers, black bears, and gray wolves, whose population estimates reach as high as 3,000, the highest in the continental United States.

Formerly occupying 18 million acres, the western and southwestern prairies are now mere shadows of their former selves, most having succumbed to extensive agricultural development. Still, the eerie booming sound made by prairie chickens is heard in the spring, along with the calls of pheasants, godwits, bobolinks, meadowlarks, and many other species. Badgers and coyotes still patrol the grasslands, looking for rodents.

Much of the original hardwood forests that extended from the southeastern to the southwestern corners of the state were cleared by Euro-American settlers, but extensive old stands of sugar maple, elm, basswood, and oak persist, providing brilliant pockets of color in autumn. Barred owls, foxes, bears, skunks, raccoons, and wild turkeys dwell in these woods.

Enlightened wildlife management practices by state and federal agencies have allowed Minnesota's wildlife to flourish. Bald eagles, once threatened by pesticides like DDT, are now so numerous that they nest in the heart of the Twin Cities. White-tailed deer and timber wolf populations are once again healthy. Peregrine falcons and trumpeter swans are other examples of species brought back from the brink.

ABOVE: A red-tailed hawk subdues a rodent in a snowy field. Redtails have excellent eyesight and can spot small prey from hundreds of feet away.

FACING PAGE: A red fox patrols a snow-covered wetland in search of mice, rabbits, or pheasants.

In the course of preparing this book, I have come to appreciate even more the extraordinary biodiversity that Minnesota is blessed with, and it is with great pride that I call this state home. This book is dedicated, with immense gratitude, to all the state agencies and individuals who, over the years, have allowed me access to private or restricted locations to obtain photographs. In so doing, they have helped me deepen my knowledge of nature.

ABOVE: A female ruby-throated hummingbird sips nectar from a trumpet vine blossom. These diminutive birds, the most abundant summer resident "hummer" in Minnesota, can flap their wings an amazing fifty-three beats per second.

RIGHT: The gray tree frog is one of fourteen species of frogs and toads in Minnesota.

FACING PAGE: The bright-red plumage of a northern cardinal adds a welcome touch of color to Minnesota's dreary winter landscape. A relatively new resident to the state, its winter range is steadily expanding northward.

ABOVE: Armed with nearly 39,000 barbed quills, an adult porcupine can defend itself very effectively against most predators, including wolves and coyotes. The fisher, a large member of the weasel family, has learned to catch a porcupine by flipping it on its back and biting its soft belly.

LEFT: In late August, this shrinking Scott County wetland attracted a crowd of great egrets and great blue herons looking for fish and amphibians.

RIGHT: A bedraggled barred owl, still wet from an overnight heavy rain, sits on a birch branch at Tamarac National Wildlife Refuge. An inhabitant of dense hardwood and coniferous forests, the barred owl is famous for its *who-cooks-for-you-who-cooks-for-you-all* call.

BELOW: The snapping turtle, Minnesota's largest turtle, is well known for its feisty disposition. The "smile" on this female that is laying eggs at Tamarac National Wildlife Refuge belies her true intention. She was actually hissing loudly at the photographer.

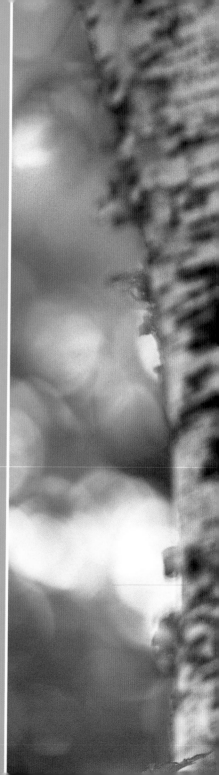

ABOVE: An American coot stretches its wings in a cattail marsh. During the fall migration, coots will assemble in large rafts of several thousand individuals. Equipped with relatively short wings, coots must run along the surface of the water in order to gain enough speed to take flight.

RIGHT: A cluster of Canada goose eggs sits comfortably in a nest lined with down plucked from the female's breast.

LEFT: In early spring, a male ruffed grouse advertises his presence to nearby females by standing on a decaying fallen log to "drum." Inaccurately called drumming, the sound is the result of a vacuum created by the forceful backstrokes of the bird's cupped wings.

RIGHT: In midsummer, the white-tailed deer's antlers are still covered in soft velvet. When antlers stop growing and harden, bucks will quickly scrape off the dried velvet by rubbing their antlers against saplings.

BELOW: A northern leopard frog basks in shallow water in Tamarac Lake in northwestern Minnesota. A female can lay up to 6,000 eggs, which she attaches to aquatic vegetation.

ABOVE: Of the two species of chipmunks found in Minnesota, the eastern (gray) chipmunk pictured here has one white stripe on each side of its body; the least chipmunk has two white stripes on each side. These small rodents favor woodpiles, brushy areas, and stone walls where they can find cover, give birth, and cache food.

FACING PAGE: This green heron in late summer plumage has just caught a dragonfly.

ABOVE: A gray tree frog searches among delicate wild rose petals for insects to eat. Excellent climbers, the frogs are equipped with large toe pads that allow them to cling to surfaces as smooth as a windowpane.

RIGHT: A remarkable swimmer, the mink is a small but fearsome predator whose prey includes fish, frogs, muskrats, and waterfowl.

ABOVE: A trumpeter swan cranes its neck to survey the marsh in the fall. Swans eat primarily aquatic vegetation, such as arrowhead tubers, wild rice, and bulrushes, which their long necks allow them to reach in water as deep as four feet.

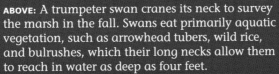

LEFT: Minnesota has the largest wolf population in the lower forty-eight states, possibly reaching 3,000.

ABOVE: In spite of its "bad guy" image derived from its bullying habits both at the birdfeeder and of vandalizing other birds' nests, the blue jay still remains the favorite of many bird lovers for its stunning plumage.

ABOVE: In early fall, a male eastern bluebird briefly pauses atop an abandoned nest, possibly that of a goldfinch. Bluebirds nest in natural tree holes but will readily accept nesting boxes.

RIGHT: A bull moose in full rutting condition peers through a thick stand of willows. The moose breeding season spans from mid-September to mid-October. Some of the best places to see moose include Agassiz National Wildlife Refuge and the Boundary Waters Canoe Area Wilderness.

ABOVE, TOP: Perhaps the prettiest duck in North America, a drake wood duck slices the surface of Minnehaha Creek. Once threatened by unregulated hunting as well as destruction of wetland habitat, its numbers have rebounded nicely thanks in part to the introduction of artificial nesting boxes. The wood duck is a dabbling duck, or surface feeder, that favors swamps, lakes, and slow-moving rivers bordered by old-growth forests.

ABOVE, BOTTOM: A female common merganser swims along the bank of the Mississippi River near Monticello. Mergansers dive to pursue and catch fish underwater. Their beaks are more narrow than a duck's.

FACING PAGE: River otters are large, semi-aquatic furbearers weighing up to thirty pounds. They feed on fish, amphibians, and crayfish; their habitat is always associated with clean lakes, streams, ponds, or rivers. These playful creatures will often approach a canoe, much to the delight of the paddlers.

ABOVE: A mallard drake stretches its wings on a frozen stretch of the Mississippi in late winter. Insulating feathers and an unusual circulatory system in their feet reduce heat loss and help ducks survive frigid conditions.

RIGHT: Bathed in late afternoon light, a flock of white pelicans preens at Agassiz National Wildlife Refuge in northwestern Minnesota. Breeding colonies of several thousand birds now exist on Lac qui Parle and Lake of the Woods—a grand success story because they had been extirpated from the state in the late 1800s.

ABOVE: Minnesota's state bird, the common loon, sits on a nest at Tamarac National Wildlife Refuge. The quintessential symbol of wilderness, this extraordinary diver favors clear, deep lakes, where it pursues fish underwater by sight. Its webbed feet, located far in back of its body, help propel it at considerable speed underwater but cause it to walk awkwardly on land.

FACING PAGE: This black bear sow seeks respite from the summer heat and mosquitoes in the fork of an aspen tree at the Vince Shute Bear Wildlife Sanctuary in St. Louis County, near Orr.

ABOVE, TOP: Piping plovers are an endangered species in Minnesota, with fewer than a handful of nests recorded in the state. They frequent sandy beaches of isolated islands in Lake of the Woods County in the extreme northern part of the state.

ABOVE, BOTTOM: Easily distinguished by its namesake chestnut-colored neck, this red-necked grebe was photographed in a breeding colony on Lake Osakis in west-central Minnesota, which it shares with western and Clark's grebes as well as Forster's and black terns.

FACING PAGE: This badger checks out the view outside its burrow. A denizen of plains and prairies, badgers are stocky and powerful. Their large front claws allow them to dig out and catch the rodents they feed on, including ground squirrels and pocket gophers.

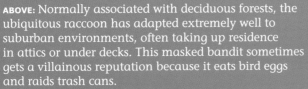

ABOVE: Normally associated with deciduous forests, the ubiquitous raccoon has adapted extremely well to suburban environments, often taking up residence in attics or under decks. This masked bandit sometimes gets a villainous reputation because it eats bird eggs and raids trash cans.

LEFT: The bobcat is a magnificent predator, considerably more common than its larger relative, the lynx. Both cats are elusive inhabitants of the thick forests of central and northern Minnesota.

ABOVE: This black-backed woodpecker has plucked the larvae of a wood-boring beetle from under the bark of a fire-scarred pine tree.

ABOVE, TOP: A timber rattlesnake warns the photographer to stay at bay by vibrating its rattle. The timber rattlesnake, sometimes called "velvet tail," is one of seventeen species of snakes in Minnesota, and one of only two species of venomous snakes in the state. It lives in the bluffs along the Mississippi River in the southwest corner of the state.

ABOVE, BOTTOM: Plodding along a sandy dune in Wabasha County in southeastern Minnesota, a Blanding's turtle searches for a suitable nest site to lay her eggs. A bright-yellow throat and high-domed shell identify this rare turtle.

FACING PAGE: Fresh out of hibernation, a woodchuck, also called a groundhog, enjoys a tasty snack of dandelion blossoms.

A female mallard (above) and trumpeter swans (right) flap their wings after thoroughly preening, or grooming, their feathers. Most waterfowl spend a considerable amount of time caring for their feathers, which serve many purposes, including insulating them from frigid winter temperatures.

LEFT: As dusk descends upon Agassiz National Wildlife Refuge, a flock of black-crowned night herons rests on dead branches before the hunt. Most active at night, these small herons feed on fish, amphibians, aquatic insects, and mollusks.

BELOW: Minnesota's most common toad, the American toad is a familiar creature and precious ally to every gardener. It eats a variety of insects and bugs it catches with its sticky tongue. Snakes are the primary predators of this toad.

ABOVE: A mourning dove (left) and a dark-eyed junco (right) endure a Minnesota snowstorm.

FACING PAGE: Once primarily a prairie dweller, the coyote has now colonized many of the state's habitats, including suburban areas, where sightings of the wild dog have increased dramatically.

ABOVE: A tom turkey struts his stuff at the edge of the woods in Crow Wing County. One of Minnesota's greatest conservation success stories, the population has expanded from just a few birds in the 1970s to more than 30,000 today.

RIGHT: Red-winged blackbirds are among the earliest birds to return to Minnesota's wetlands in the spring. This male is belting out its unmusical *o-ka-ree* to claim its territory.

LEFT AND BELOW: Each spring, male greater prairie-chickens perform elaborate courtship displays to attract females, including stomping their feet, inflating air sacks, and emitting eerie moans. Here they square off on a fog-shrouded booming ground at Bluestem Prairie Scientific Natural Area. As tallgrass prairies continue to dwindle, so does the population of these grouse of the open grasslands.

FACING PAGE: Tipping the scale at forty to fifty pounds on average, the beaver is North America's largest rodent. These superb swimmers can stay underwater for up to twenty minutes.

ABOVE: A great blue heron stalks the shallows at Wood Lake Nature Center in Richfield. Nearly four feet tall, the great blue heron will eat almost anything that comes within reach of its sharp bill, including fish, frogs, and small mammals.

LEFT: In early May near Lake Osakis, a great blue heron rookery in the uppermost branches of deciduous trees bustles with activity.

ABOVE: Irresistibly cute in fluffy yellow down, a gosling Canada goose trails its parents on a feeding foray. Goslings are able to walk and swim within hours of hatching.

RIGHT: Wrens are cavity nesters. Both the male and female actively incubate their four to six eggs and feed their hatchlings. This house wren has brought back a grasshopper to feed its hungry young.

FACING PAGE: A white-tailed deer fawn remains utterly still as the photographer approaches. Newborn fawns have no odor when first born and instinctively flatten themselves into the ground to elude predators. Does often give birth to twins.

ABOVE: Ospreys are also called "fish hawks" because they feed exclusively on fish. The birds build large, bulky nests of sticks at the top of dead trees or on man-made structures such as power lines and nesting platforms. They are most common in the lake-dotted northern tier of the state.

RIGHT: A great gray owl in the Sax-Zim Bog in northeastern Minnesota pounces on a rodent. Exceptional hunters of mice and voles, great grays can locate and catch prey beneath two feet of snow. Relatively rare visitors to Minnesota, these residents of Canada's boreal forests can "invade" the state in large numbers when the rodent populations crash on the birds' home range, such as the winter of 2005–2006, which brought thousands of great grays into Minnesota.

ABOVE: A young thirteen-lined ground squirrel munches on seeds. Often mistakenly called gophers, these active animals favor shortgrass areas that offer great visibility. Their many predators include hawks, badgers, coyotes, and snakes.

ABOVE: In a behavior typical of this species, an American bittern points its bill up to camouflage itself, all but disappearing while standing perfectly still among the dried stalks of a cattail marsh.

FACING PAGE: A muskrat grooms its fur while perched atop its lodge made of mud and marsh vegetation. Muskrats might also live in burrows they dig along the banks of lakes and rivers. Their favorite food is cattails.

ABOVE: An adult bald eagle prepares to take off from its perch near Lake Pepin. In winter, this section of the Mississippi River between Red Wing and La Crosse, Wisconsin, with its many dams and channels that remain partially open, attracts large concentrations of bald eagles—as well as visitors, who come to observe and admire the symbol of our nation.

RIGHT: A gray wolf scans the woods for signs of its main winter prey, the white-tailed deer. Occasionally even the mighty moose, weighing more than 1,000 pounds, can be brought down by a pack of these mighty hunters, although they prefer to target young or sick animals.

ABOVE: A garter snake pursues (above, top) and catches a minnow (above, bottom) along the shore of South Chippewa Lake at Tamarac National Wildlife Refuge. Its attempts were almost always successful, and the snake would bring the fish on land and swallow it headfirst.

FACING PAGE: A gray squirrel sits atop a birch stump on a cold December morning. Grays do not hibernate, remaining active in the dead of winter. The squirrel's remarkable sense of smell allows it to retrieve nuts buried under a foot of snow.

ABOVE: Two mallard drakes engage in a back-to-back preening session.

FACING PAGE: In early October at Wolsfeld Woods Scientific Natural Area, a tiger salamander crawls across the forest floor littered with colorful sugar maple leaves. The salamander will hibernate for the winter in abandoned mammal burrows that reach below the frost line.

ABOVE: American robins are a familiar sight on suburban lawns as they search for earthworms and insects. In summer and fall, they supplement their diets with fruits and berries.

ABOVE: These two great horned owlets sitting on a leafy nest in Pine County await the return of their parents to be fed. Great horned owls do not build a nest of their own but rather take over the nests of crows, hawks, or squirrels. They court in January and February and lay their eggs by March.

RIGHT: Turkey vultures are large scavengers with an almost eagle-size six-foot wingspan. During the midday hours, they can be seen soaring in wide circles, riding the warm air currents. They feed on animal carcasses.

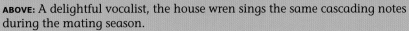

ABOVE: A delightful vocalist, the house wren sings the same cascading notes during the mating season.

FACING PAGE: In late summer, a black bear in northern Minnesota looks up briefly before resuming its search for food. Bears need to build up fat reserves before hibernating for the winter. Most of a bear's diet consists of vegetative matter, a surprising fact considering its carnivorous anatomy.

ABOVE: Weighed down by dew in the early August dawn, an adult monarch butterfly clings to a cluster of goldenrod blossoms, awaiting the warming rays of the sun. This generation of butterflies will soon undertake a 2,000-mile journey to the forests of central Mexico, where they'll spend the winter before returning north the following spring.

ABOVE: In the protective cover of bulrush and cattail beds, a western grebe chick enjoys a commanding view of Lake Osakis from its parent's back.

RIGHT: Trumpeter swans rest and mingle with Canada geese and mallards in Scott County during spring migration. They will soon head to breeding areas in northern Minnesota, Canada, or the western United States.

ABOVE: In late September, a school of pink salmon fights the swift current of the Cascade River, a tributary of Lake Superior, to reach a suitable spot to spawn.

FACING PAGE: A cloudy fall day finds this white-tailed deer buck foraging in a hardwood forest in Becker County. In early November, he will enter the rutting season.

ABOVE: Its coat soaked by morning dew, an eastern cottontail explores a suburban backyard. These prolific rabbits are no friend of the gardener; their appetites can cause extensive damage to flowerbeds or vegetable gardens.

FACING PAGE: The shorter, cooler days of autumn trigger a period of intense activity for beavers. They eat and work feverishly, cutting down trees and stockpiling branches near their lodges, to be eaten in winter when ice covers their pond.

ABOVE: Walnuts provide an energy-rich food for this red squirrel in late summer. Normally associated with northern coniferous forests, red squirrels also inhabit southern hardwood forests and suburban areas where they can find nuts, pinecones, berries, and fungi.

LEFT: A white-tailed deer doe pauses along a forest path before bolting to the safety of the woods at Tamarac National Wildlife Refuge.

ABOVE: A northern hawk owl stares down the photographer in the Sax-Zim Bog in St. Louis County. This medium-size owl is a rare but regular visitor from Canada's boreal forests. It is a voracious eater of mice, voles, and lemmings.

FACING PAGE: A very rare cat, the lynx is most at home in Minnesota's northern boreal forest along the Canadian border. Enormous feet allow it to walk in deep snow and chase its primary prey, the snowshoe hare. Cyclical highs and lows in hare populations directly determine lynx numbers in a given area.

ABOVE: With wings outstretched, a Forster's tern aggressively defends her mound nest, made of marsh vegetation.

FACING PAGE: Because of the foul-smelling spray they squirt on attackers when cornered, striped skunks have few predators other than the great-horned owl.

ABOVE: This male Canada goose, called a gander, strikes an alert pose as he stands guard near his nest while his mate is incubating their eggs. The loud *a-honk* of Canada geese returning home from their wintering grounds in March is a welcome sound to many a winter-weary Minnesotan.

ABOVE: Sandhill cranes are silhouetted against the sky at sundown as they return to roost in a wetland for the night. Cranes are often mistaken for herons. In flight it's easy to differentiate them: Cranes fly with their necks and legs fully extended, and herons fly with their necks cocked in an **S** shape.

RIGHT: Sunrise finds trumpeter swans huddled together on the Mississippi River in 25 below zero weather.

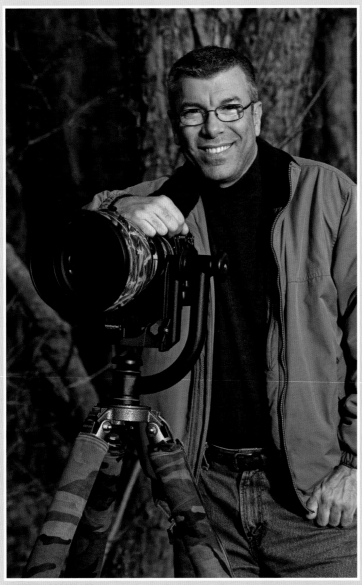

Dominique Braud is currently pursuing a dual career as a nature photographer and a full-time high school teacher in Apple Valley, Minnesota. A native of France, he holds graduate degrees in humanities from the University of Poitiers and the University of Iowa. He specializes in wildlife and scenic images of Minnesota but also has traveled extensively from Central America to the Arctic Circle to photograph his subjects. His work has been widely published through stock photo agencies, and his credits include books, calendars, and publications such as *Birder's World, National Wildlife, Ranger Rick*, and *Outdoor Photographer*. For over a decade, Dominique was a contract photographer for the U.S. Fish and Wildlife Service's Tamarac National Wildlife Refuge in Minnesota. He has written more than fifty articles and currently writes and illustrates a regular nature column for *Lake Country Journal Magazine* in Brainerd, Minnesota. He lives in Farmington, Minnesota.